THE GOLDEN BOOK OF
MARRAKESH

Text by
ENNIO MACCONI

Photos by
ANDREA PISTOLESI

Raimage
Raissouni Image

BONECHI

INDEX

History of the Imperial city ....*Page* 3

Arab fantasias, dances, and folklore .... " 7
City center .... " 12
Dar Si Said Museum .... " 60

GARDENS .... " 81
-Agdal .... " 86
-Majorelle .... " 84
-Menara .... " 81

Hotel Mamounia .... " 90
Modern city .... " 88

MOROCCAN CRAFTS .... " 68
-Objects for the home, copper and pottery .... " 74
-Wood .... " 71

MOSQUES
-el-Mansouria .... " 16
-Ben Youssef .... " 46
-Koutoubia .... " 11

PALACES
-al-Badi .... " 25
-Bahia .... " 30
-Convention Center .... " 89
-Royal .... " 42

Place Djemaa el-Fna .... " 51
Saadian Tombs .... " 19

SOUKS .... " 64
-Carpets .... " 67
-Leather workers .... " 67
-Wool .... " 72

Walls and Gates .... " 14

Outskirts
-The Palmeraie .... " 92
-Ouzoud Falls .... " 94

Distributeur: RAIMAGE Sarl., Angle Rues de Russie et Emsallah, Tél.: 93 42 02, Tanger, Maroc.

© Copyright by CASA EDITRICE BONECHI, Via Cairoli, 18/b Florence - Italy
E-mail: bonechi@bonechi.it   Internet: www.bonechi.it

Text by Ennio Macconi
Printed in Italy by Centro Stampa Editoriale Bonechi
Translated by Erika Pauli for Studio Comunicare Florence.
The photographs are the property of the Archives of the Casa Editrice Bonechi and were taken by ANDREA PISTOLESI

ISBN 88-8029-250-1

* * *

On this and the following page, two pictures of the buildings and mosques that overlook Place Djemaa el-Fna.

HISTORY OF THE IMPERIAL CITY

In its nine centuries of life Marrakesh alternated moments of splendor and glory with long years of obscurity. It was built and destroyed more than once, plundered and embellished, venerated and punished. Thre are few cities in the world whose history is so closely tied to that of their country, to the point of even bearing the same name. Marrakesh still today bears witness to the past splendor of its troubled and fascinating history and is to all effects a museum-city, with its striking mosques, minarets, splendid palaces, gardens which seem miraculously to spring from a void in the dry thirsty earth, where they were created thanks to the genius and fantasy of its builders. There is something both thrilling and delightful in the ancient lanes, the crooks and crannies, the shops of the souk where everything can be had; but there is also something overwhelming in the feeling of infinity of the landscapes stretching back towards the mountains of the High Atlas, the vastness of this mythical square (Place Djemaa el-Fna), the spectacular geometry of its walls.

Marrakesh was once the capital of all Morocco, an imperial city on a par with Fez, Meknès and Rabat. It was and is the capital of the South: with its burning sunsets and red and pink houses, an infinite variety of aromas and the perfumes of spices and acute and sweet essences; the intoxicating scents of roses and jasmine; the spell cast by the songs and words of the craftsmen and the snake charmers; the sound of water and the milling crowds in the markets; the majestic silence of its Berber and Arab art treasures; the incredible snows on the mountain peaks overlooking the city.

It sprang up as a great Berber metropolis, a symbol of the pride of this nomad race, accustomed to a hard life bounded by the sea of the Sahara sands and the friendless rugged stones of the Atlas mountain chain and its snow-covered peaks, and that is what it will always be. No one - neither the Phoenicians nor the

Romans, the Byzantines nor the Vandals - ever succeeded in completely dominating this pride. And not even the Arabs when they began their conquests in the seventh century.

Today Marrakesh is a city with over 500,000 inhabitants, the third in Morocco, after Rabat and Casablanca, the principal city of a province which numbers a population of over 1,260,000 souls. It is the principal crossroads for the Saharian south, beyond the High Atlas and for the routes which lead to Agadir, Casablanca, Fez and Meknès. It is, in other words, an ideal bridge which joins the north of Morocco to the south. The principal activity consists of crafts (leather, copper, textiles, carpets), in which 58.5% of the inhabitants are employed. But Marrakesh, in the seventies and eighties and now more than ever, thanks to its systems of hotels which cater to all pockets and range from the simplest to the most luxurious with splendid swimming pools, casino and perfect 18-hole golf courses, has consolidated its role as capital of Moroccan tourism, competing, perhaps, only with Agadir and its blue sea.

The almost millenary history of Marrakesh has always been closely related to that of the principal Berber tribes and their encounter-clash with Islam: the Almoravids, the Almohads, the Merinids, the Saadians, the Alaouites. Uncertainty still surrounds the origins of what was to become the capital of the Berber empire and its culture. Some date its foundation to 1062, others to 1070/71. But there are no doubts as to the fact that it was Abu Bakr who first established a settlement in Marrakesh in the bowl of the Haouz (which stretches for almost 6000 sq. km. at the feet of the High Atlas). The nucleus of a first casbah (Ksar al-Hajer) is also attributed to him.

With him the Almoravids became great and so did Marrakesh. In the next forty years, that initial temporary camp, called Marrakesh ("go away quickly") became the capital of a real empire, that ranged from Algeria to the Atlantic, from the Sahara to the Ebro. Yusuf ibn-Tashfin had the first large mosque built almost immediately, which the subsequent lords of the city later destroyed. He set out to making Marrakesh a true metropolis. The city, which lacked water, was furnished with an ingenious system of subterranean conduits, the khettara, still in existence today, which connect the various wells discovered in the area that stretches out at the base of the rocky hills of the Gueliz. But Yusuf ibn-Tashfin was a Berber and a man of the desert, and once he had found water, he set about creating a sort of miracle, a palmeraie or palm grove. Legend narrates that his soldiers, who ate great quantities of dates, contributed to its creation by throwing the pits on the sand. But his genius was truly realized in his military undertakings.

He took over the regions of the north, from Tangiers to the eastern part of what is now Algeria. He crossed the Strait of Gibraltar to lend a hand to the Muslim princes in Spain threatened by the Christianity of Alfonso VI of Castille. In a merry go round of events and alliances, he ended up by ruling the lands of Malaga, Granada, Cordoba, Seville, as far as Valencia. These forty years of expansion were to leave an indelible mark in the future history of Marrakesh and all Morocco. For the city which was in a phase of growth it was the occasion to assimilate the Spanish and Moorish cultures as well as the classic Arab culture.

When Yusuf ibn-Tashfin died in 1106, he was succeeded by his son Ali, who continued his father's commitments. In just one year the first part of the great circle of city walls which still today encloses the medina, the oldest part of the city, was built. But at the same time Marrakesh was acquiring the features of a mercantile and craft city, with the working of wood and leather.

From then on the fortunes of the "Berber capital", at this point Arab in its main features, were to be the fruit of the vicissitudes and struggles which rewarded or destroyed the various ethnic groups who appeared on the scene. There were to be only four Almoravid sovereigns. At the end, Ishaq, the last and almost still a child, was decapitated by the new lords, the Almoravids. Only 41 years after the death of its founder, Marrakesh was captured by Ibn Tumart. It was March 23, 1147 when the hordes of Almohad horsemen, prey to a new furor of religious reform, took over the city. These were dramatic days. Marrakesh was laid waste; the Almoravids were decimated, imprisoned, forced to take flight.

The new order of the "Unitarians" (which is what Almohad means), with Ibn Tumart who had proclaimed himself Mahdi (sent by God), once more launched the religious idea of divine unity, and put this into practice by cancelling all that the Almoravids had done. And only after having demolished, did reconstruction begin. Ruins were left behind, and now came the moment for new masterworks. Abd al-Mumin, the real founder of the dynasty, built the first Koutoubia, and then another one (the one now there), new gardens and large pools for water. His successor, Abu Yakub Yusuf even created a new quarter and may have begun the splendid garden of the Agdal or Aguedal. Yakub al-Mansur (the "victorious") in 1185 began building a new casbah, endowed the city with hospitals, filled the medina with a dozen superb palaces. For the Almohads and Marrakesh it was a moment of new splendor. The dynasty was to reign for almost a century. The city became a first class cultural center, humanist and scientific, with astronomers, mathematicians and philosophers of fame such as Averröes called to the court.

Then, once again, the crisis. A decline that began in Spain, with the great defeat inflicted by the Christian armies of Alfonso VII in 1212 at Las Navas de Tolosa. Repercussions of the rout were transformed into years of anarchy. At the end the Merinids, a nomad Berber peoples who came from the Sahara, saw their chance. Marrakesh was occupied in 1269 and the last Almohad sovereign swept away. The new rulers moved their capital to Fez.

Ups and downs were a matter of course in this city, a stage at all times for the political and relgious contrasts which saw peoples and tribes from the entire Maghreb opposing each other in the name of Islam. The pomp of the periods of the Almoravids and the Almohads seemed a thing of the distant past. The Merinids were never able to construct empires of this sort, while the Christian penetration on the coasts of Morocco gathered force with the arrival of the Portuguese. The entire thirteenth and fourteenth centuries were nothing but one vicissitude after another, leaving for history and for their descendants practically nothing but the undertakings of Ibn Batuta, the great traveler (a kind of Merinid Marco Polo) whose travels took him to Peking, Samarcand, Timbuctu. These were the years of a Morocco split in two parts and of a Marrakesh which tried in vain to recuperate a national hegemony.

After the interval of Wattasid power, new splendors had to await the arrival of a new and great dynasty, that of the Saadians. They dominated events of the sixteenth century, gaining force and power as they succeeded in standing up to the Christian penetration in the north and then pushing into the great south. The Saadian renaissance, a new golden age for Marrakesh, took shape with Moulay Abdallah who restored the casbah, created a Mellah (a Hebrew "ghetto" in the old city), built a great medrassa, raised the Moussain mosque. Ahmed al-Mansur (el Dehbi, the "golden one", the most famous, 1578-1603) in particular had splendid masterworks such as the al-Badi palace (only ruins now remain) and the Saadian tombs built.

The Saadians, the "sherifs" (descendants of Mohammed), once more exploited the springs of religious sentiment, intolerance against the danger of the "infidel", the desire for order and tranquility after years of uncertainties. The renewal of the fortunes of Marrakesh coincided with those of Morocco as a whole, firmly under Saadian control, and the direct consequence was the expansion of commerce, to the point of giving Morocco the reputation of being a "land of gold".

By the middle of the seventeenth century the powerful Saadians also began to decline. For the glorious "Berber capital" it seemed to be a replay of previous events. The new lords, the Alaouites, the same dynasty which still reigns over Morocco with Hassan II, transferred the centers of their power. Moulay er Rachid transferred the capital to Fez.

Not until the end of the nineteenth century, with Moulay Hassan (1873-1894) and his son Moulay Abd al-Aziz, was there a return of a period of prosperity for the ancient "capital of the south". The Bahia palace was built (1895-1901), and the Dar Si Said palace.

With the twentieth century Morocco too found itself involved in clashes with European colonialism, above all French and Spanish. Marrakesh was still to be the protagonist of important events. In the years of French penetration, in 1907, Moulay Abd al-Hafid had himself proclaimed sultan of Morocco, in Marrakesh, and his place was then taken by El Hiba, the great insurgent of the Moroccan south, who took up arms against the French. But on September 7, 1912, the troups of the French Colonel Mangin occupied the city where Moulay Abd al-Hafiz, the famous Glaoui, was to remain as uncontrasted lord and pasha, thanks to the support he had supplied to the new French protectorate.

This power was to last until the independence of Morocco (March 2, 1956) and the advent to the throne of the sovereign of the new national unity, Mohammed V, father of the present monarch, Hassan II.

The Marrakesh of today is also the fruit of the difficult years of the French protectorate. And it was the French, with the occupation of the city in 1912, who built the new part, the Gueliz, three km. northeast of the old medina. Since then expansion has been going on continuously. The old city protected within its walls has remained intact in its age-old charm, while new quarters were added to the initial French agglomerates. Further urban expansion marked the fifties and sixties and the population of the city has more than quadrupled since the beginning of this century.

So that now the "Berber capital" is both a city of the past, a precious coffer of centuries of history, art and culture, and a great metropolis of contemporary Morocco, a unique country in Africa, a melting pot and crossroads for the black continent, the Arab world and Europe.

ARAB FANTASIAS, DANCES AND FOLKLORE

At least once, before leaving Marrakesh and Morocco, it is well worth it to go and see a "Fantasia". Of all the fascinating, mysterious and evocative culture of this country, with such an extraordinary wealth of history, art and folk traditions, one of the most thrilling moments is the "fantasia", a mad furious race with highly-skilled horsemen charging full gallop and whirling long slender rifles in the air as if they were scimitars.

If you are lucky enough to see one, you cannot help but be carried away by the shouting, volleys of rifle shots, sudden flashes as the men lean out of their saddles seemingly defying the laws of gravity; nor will you ever forget the excitement of watching the Berber horses, not particularly large, but strong and tough, as they cross each other's paths, almost collide, and then take off again at full speed in a cloud of black and yellow dust.

Horsemen wield long scimitars and the "moukkala", the splendid long-barreled, finely inlaid rifles, while musicians on the outskirts of the field beat their drums in Berber folk rhythms.

*This is what a "Fantasia" looks like, as riders charge
wildly down on their horses.*

The long rifles, the moukkala, carried by the riders
are of great beauty. Many are still old models with a
flint lock mechanism, and the butts are encrusted
with ivory, silver and gold, in a variety of shapes.
Every tribe had its own. Each rider must also have
his powder flask in leather, or heavy fabric, always
embroidered. And curved razor-sharp daggers are
worn in the wide belts of these riders of the wind.
Sometimes the fantasias last hours. Their roots go
back in history and in the tradition of the moussem
(the pilgrimages to the tombs of the saints which,
once the religious part of the ceremony was over,
gave way to the festivals, the "charges"). Another
occasion for the fantasias are the great gatherings
celebrating the various festivals, such as the date
festival (in October at Erfoud) or the cherry and rose
festival. But they are also organized for the ram
festival (in the month chosen for the pilgrimage to
the Mecca) or for the Aid es Seghir, the end of
Ramadan, or for the Mulud, the anniversary of the
birth of the Prophet Mohammed (born around 570
in the Mecca, who died in Medina in 632).
Any mention of dances also means adventuring into
the magical world of music and of sounds, of
instruments and spell-binding rhythms, the fruit of
the Berber tradition and their subsequent encounter
with the Islamic culture. A superb opportunity
awaits those lucky enough to be in Marrakesh for
the national Festival, held every year in the
beginning of June in the evocative ruins of the al-
Badi palace. Music and dance are part of daily life
of the Morocco of yesterday and today. No occasion, sad or happy, is without the accompaniment
of instruments and dance. And in this too the Arab
culture has wedded, mixed with, has joined itself
with the Berber tradition.
Up to the point where it becomes impossible to
distinguish Berbers from Arabs, by now all alike for
the racial group of both is Caucasoid. For the
primordial Berbers, the mythical peoples who in the
very beginning inhabited the fantastic continent of
Atlantis, music and dance were of fundamental
importance in a cultural tradition which was
entrusted to the oral tradition, rather than to writing.
The instruments of the dance and song vary from
the terracotta drums with a muted sound, whose
voices are changed by heating the skins at the
bonfires, to the ghembà, a small three-stringed
guitar, to the shrill-voiced flutes, with the often
obsessive underlying background sounds of
clapping hands, stressing, keeping time to the
movements and words.

The most famous dance, originally from Ouarzazate and the linguistic zone of Taselhit (south-western Morocco, comprising a square which includes the western and central Atlas, the Sous valley and the Anti Atlas) may be the Hawas, known also as "Berber opera". Up to two hundred persons take part and at the end the rhythms and situations are of collective frenzy. Generally a great fire is lit at the center of the casbah. The men take place on one side with the women in a semicircle. A man in the center directs the dances and the sound, while the women invoke God, with undulating frenetic movements. In the Tamazigt language area, one of the Berber dialects, another collective dance, the ahidus, has become popular. The principal identifying feature is the participation of the women with shrill shrieks. Of particular note is the Guedra (the name of an amphora covered with a skin), a desert dance, danced by a single woman. The woman kneels in the center of a circle of men, often wearing a large dark cloak. Generally she is very young, with a black veil which however does not cover her face and with silver jewelry braided into her hair. She will continue as if obsessed, with a crescendo of movments of her hips, body, hands, until suddenly she stops. The groups of dancers, the Gnawa, who perform in Place Djemaa el-Fna are also of African, in particular Sudanese, origin.

The best way to get at least an idea of Moroccan folklore, of the ensemble of folk traditions and their manifestations is that of calmy enjoying the endless show to be found in Place Djemaa el-Fna and in the many souk of the Kissaria, the old center of the market city, inside the medina, which once was closed at night by heavy gates. For here everything speaks of the traditions, customs and usages that are still alive today: from the splendid cuisine, to the dress of men and women, to the craft objects, the layout of the houses where every space, every garden, every door, every water basin, every fountain has its antique meaning.

And it is in the square that you will also find the famous snake charmers, signs of a cult which calls to mind influences of old that go back as far as India. But there is another legend which explains the origin of one of the most ancient traditions of Moroccan craftwork: that of the carpets, with their lovely colors and designs. The story goes that a stork, in far off days, let fall on a Moroccan house a piece of carpet which had been woven in Asia Minor, a land that was practically out of reach. Ever since then, the women who found it have been weaving carpets, one finer than the other.

Few peoples in the world have been able to collect the experiences of their history as have the Berbers and make them live once more, transforming or completely assimilating them, and at the same time maintaining their own individual identity.

KOUTOUBIA

There is no point on the horizon from which you cannot see the minaret of the Koutoubia. In the heart of the historical medina (with the mosque of the same name by its side), it is the symbol of Marrakesh, together with the immense area of Place Djemaa el-Fna just around the corner.

The minaret, like the mosque, is one of the jewels of Almohad art, built for Abd al-Mumin and finished by Yakub al-Mansur (between 1184 and 1189).

Access to the highest terrace is forbidden, but on crystal clear days, the peaks of the Azafi, 30 km. away are visible. The measurements of the minaret are imposing, but well balanced and carefully studied up to the last centimeter. The basic relationship between width and height is 1 to 5. And while the side measures 12.80 meters, the height shoots up (and these are the only words to use even in regards to other minarets of comparable height) to 77 meters, considering the highest point (69 if you stop at the skylight).

From the outside too, the minaret is always something to be seen, whatever the hour of the day. The pink sandstone, from quarries once opened in the hills surrounding Gueliz, changes color as the sunbeams strike it at different angles with the passing of the day, as if it were a gigantic torch. The entire construction is dominated at the top by three spheres of varying sizes, ranging from a few centimeters in diameter, to almost 2 meters. The three spheres, which also glow in the rays of the sun, are in gilded copper. A legend however says that they were made by melting down the gold jewellery of the wife of Yakub al-Mansur.

To keep them from being stolen, a magic spell supposedly forced some geni to keep watch over them. Anyone who approached the globes with evil intentions, would thus find the geni waiting for him. On the outside, each side of the construction is different, with floral ornaments, majolica borders and painting on plaster. Inside, the building consists of six rooms, one above the other, which are in communication not so much by actual flights of stairs as by a sort of rising ramp. On the top part, the terrace which goes all around the minaret is decorated by a series of crenellations, two meters high.

The Mosque stands north of the minaret. The first mosque was destroyed for some unknown reason, but it is to be presumed that it had been built in an

Three pictures of the Koutoubia mosque, a stone's throw from Place Djemaa el-Fna, with the famous minaret, symbol of the city, 77 meters high, a jewel of Almohad art.

The three globes at the top of the minaret recall the three basic principles of Islam: Faith, Prayer and Fasting.

incorrect position, obviously with respect to the Mecca. What we see today, also built for Abd el-Mumin, is considered a real pearl of Almohad art. It follows the famous "T-shape" of the mosque of Kairouan and is a compendium of Almohad architectural concepts: tile facing; T-shaped plan, with an aisle parallel to the back wall, on which the most numerous and decorated domes rise up. The Almohads also chose this style for the great mosque of Hassan in Rabat, begun in 1195 but never finished.

The Mosque of the Koutoubia (only Muslims are permitted to enter), known as the "book venders' mosque" (more than 200 book stores stand around the base), was also built, like the minaret, with stone quarried in the Gueliz.

Inside it is divided into 17 aisles perpendicular to the wall which marks the back end and on which is to be found the only transversal aisle (the one which intersects with the other 17 aisles and gives the plan its typical T-shape). There are two pulpits in carved wood, also Almohad work, thought to be among the finest examples of this type in Islam. Just when construction began remains problematical. It seems most likely that it was the year in which it was opened to worship: 1158.

THE CITY CENTER

The adventure inside Marrakesh and its most fascinating zones begins along this traffic-choked artery; cars, busses, carriages, men and women on foot all moving towards Place Djemaa el-Fna, the heart of the Medina, beyond the ancient walls and the gates. This is the pulsating heart of the metropolis of today, with behind it, to the northwest, the hills of the Gueliz, the first of the new districts, which began to take shape around the twenties, and which is characterized by its broad boulevards, shaded by perfumed jacaranda trees and jasmine, with palaces and buildings of a modern capital, of a city no longer looking at its past but racing to keep up with the rhythms of contemporary life. The spacious Avenue Mohammed V passes here, along which the most important bus lines run (including one which goes directly from the Gueliz to Place Djemaa el-Fna). This is the principal artery of Marrakesh, almost a "throughway" which runs through the city from northwest to southeast, and peters out at the foot of the Koutoubia. No one can say they have really been in Marrakesh unless they have been taken around at least once by one of the countless

No matter what the time of day a long endless river of people on foot, in carriages, on busses and cars, clogs up the heart of the city, Avenue Mohammed V, which connects the Gueliz directly to the "grande place".

The minaret of the Koutoubia, proud and imposing, overlooks Place Djemaa el-Fna.

*The walls and the gates are one of the most charactric elements of the landscape of Marrakesh.
The walls were begun in 1126 by Ali ibn-Yusuf, an Almoravid, son of the founder of the city.
The principal gates, of which there are 14, lead into the Medina. Photo above: the Bab Agnaou.*

ubiquitous horse-drawn carriages (except in the souks, where the best way is on foot). Really beginning our visit of Marrakesh, means discovering the three main zones of the city, all enclosed in the medina, the old part, protected by the walls (with a perimeter of about 15 km.), entry to which is through the dozen principal gates. In addition to the tombs of the seven patron saints of the city, the northern part, the historical medina at its best, holds the Ben Yusuf mosque. Originally Almoravid, the koubba is all that remains of the original building which was restructured in the sixteenth and then in the nineteenth century. The Ben Yusuf medrassa, considered the most important Koran school in the entire Maghreb, with its bronze door, its great internal basin, and the splendors of its courtyard is located next to the mosque. The world of the souk lies in wait for the visitor in the heart of the Medina, beginning with Place Djemaa el-Fna and adventuring into the thousand twisting lanes as far as the ancient kissaria (the old "corridors" of the oldest market center), going from the carpet souk to that of jewellery, from the souk of the dyers, an entire street where the sky is closed off by skeins of cloth hung up to dry on wooden lattices, and where the light filters through, in ever changing plays of light. To the south, in the monumental part of the medina around the Bab Agnaou, lie the palaces of

the great dynasties which made Marrakesh a capital and an imperial city: the Bahia palace; what remains of the al-Badi palace; the royal palace, the Saadian tombs.

THE WALLS AND THE GATES

The walls are one of the most characteristic features of the city. They were begun in 1126 by Ali ibn-Yusuf of the Almoravid dynasty, son of the founder of Marrakesh, Yusuf ibn-Tashfin, who had died twenty years earlier.

They were supposed to defend the city from attack but turned out to be useless when the Almohads plundered the city and took it over on March 23, 1147. The walls, which were subsequently enlarged as the city spread out, are almost 15 km. long. In building them the Almoravids and then the Almohads made use of a clay and lime mixture, the "tabia", a sort of red mud, and the limestone material they could find in the hills of the Gueliz. The height varies along the perimeter from 5.6 to 9 meters and they range in width from one and a half to two meters. A story about the building of the

The walls.

walls that sounds more like legend has also come down to us. According to this tale, the astronomers of the time said building should be begun in a period when the moon was at a certain point in the sky. To trace out the ground plan, ropes were arranged on the ground, forming a large square. This was to have been the perimeter on which the walls were to rise, but not before the cords moved by themselves. By chance, the story goes, a crow perched on one of the cords one day, making it move and deceiving the men who were waiting for the propitious moment to begin work. So the fact that the walls were never truly strong and impregnable is all the fault of that crow.

The fourteen gates leading into the medina are set in the walls at irregular intervals: Bab Erraha; Bab Doukkala; Bab el-Khemis; Debbagh; Aylen; Aghmat; Ahmar; Ighli; Ksiba; Agnaou; er-Robb; Echcharia; el-Jadid; el-Makhzen.

Among the most important are the Bab Doukkala, built by the Almoravids, on the west, the first encountered going northwards; the Bab el-Khemis or "Thursday gate", or "gate of Fez", with two bastions and overlooking the characteristic donkey market, held on Thursdays; the Bab Debbagh, also known for the panorama to be had climbing up the terrace and which provides an overall view of the tanners' streets and courts, full of skins and the typical tubs where the leather is dyed. Moving southwards is the Bab Aghmat, known in history because it was through here that on March 23, 1147 the Almohads succeeded in entering the city and conquering it. The next gate, the Bab Ahmar, the "red gate", looks towards the splendid gardens of the kagdal. The story attached to the Bab er-Robb is sad for in 1308 the Merinid sultan, Abu Thabit, had the heads of 600 of his opposers hung here on its crenellations, after a ferocious repression. The Bab el-Jadid, which leads directly to the famous Hotel Mamounia and into Place Youssef ibn Tashfin was the last to be opened in the wall, in 1915. The finest of all, at the entrance to the casbah, is the Bab Agnaou, which leads to the Saadian tombs, and was built in 1150 by Sultan Abd al-Mumin. Considered a jewel of Almohad architecture, the name is a mispronounciation of an old Berber name, agnaw, or negro, even if the literal meaning is "he who speaks a foreign tongue". And it is from this gate that one reaches the casbah erected by Yakub el-Mansur in the twelfth century

EL-MANSOURIA MOSQUE

The mosque of the casbah stands on the left after entering by the Bab Agnaou. A narrow corridor on the right leads straight to the entrance of the Saadian tombs.

The mosque of the casbah is also known as el-Mansouria, after its builder, Yakub al-Mansur, the "victorious", third sovereign of the Almohad dynasty, who became famous for having defeated the Christians in Spain, was considered the founder of Rabat and committed himself to beautifying Marrakesh, endowing it among other things with a new casbah with twelve palaces, a hospital and gardens as well as completing the works of the Giralda, begun by his father, in Seville.

It was to beautify his casbah in Marrakesh that he had the new mosque erected between 1185 and 1190. The building we see today, in part destroyed by a fire in 1574, is the fruit of two later transformations by the Saadian Sultan Moulay Abdellah (1557-1574) and the Alaouite Prince Sidi Mohammed ben Abdellah (1757-1790), who set his hands to it when he was his father's caliph.

The mosque is a building of considerable size with a facade 80 meters long crowned by brackets and crenellation. The interior decoration is rather sober. The ground plan is in the classical T-shape and has eleven aisles. The ceilings are of painted wood; the minbar, a sort of thirteenth-century pulpit, is also in wood, with ivory inlays, and the doors are sheathed in bronze lamina.

Outside, the spacious central court is flanked by four smaller ones.

The entire construction is crowned by the minaret which rises to the sky, and is also of considerable size and with the upper part marked by blue-ground majolica decorations. As was the case with the Koutoubia, there is a story involving the copper spheres at the top of this minaret which were to have been in gold, the gold of the jewels of Yakub al-Mansur's wife

The el-Mansouria mosque, or mosque of the casbah, seen from the outside, lies but a few steps from the Bab Agnaou and the entrance to the Saadian tombs. The marvelous minaret is decorated with blue majolicas and culminates in three spheres, which a legend says are of gold.

SAADIAN TOMBS

This is one of the most haunting sites in the city. The way there leads through a narrow corridor next to the mosque of the casbah. The tombs date to the late sixteenth century, but it was not until 1917, when the great wall built a century later by the Alaouite Sultan Moulay Ismail was torn down, that they were discovered and opened to the greater public.

The Saadian Sultan Moulay Ahmed al-Mansur (1574-1603) had intended them to be seen as we see them today in the form of a small cemetery. After the death of his mother, Lalla Messaouda, in 1591, and her burial here, he decided to organize the grounds in this form. Before that the Merinid Sultan Abu el-Hassan had already found burial here in 1351, as well as a Saadian prince, Mohammed ech-Cheick, in 1557.

The tombs have been arranged in two separate mausoleums which overlook a garden. The main mausoleum, to the south, with a splendid door of finely carved cedarwood, consists of three separate rooms. The first, the room of the mihrab, the prayer niche oriented towards the Mecca, is characterized by an oratory with three aisles and three arcades which rest on four marble columns. A finely worked door leads to the actual funerary room. Above and below, on the right and on the left, the eye is drawn incessantly from one marvel to another: inlaid cedarwood, ceilings with precious "stalactites", a soft diffused light that envelops and highlights everything. The main tomb in this room is that of the Alaouite Sultan Moulay el-Yazid (1790-1792), a child, just as the other tombs to be seen here are also of children.

But it is the second room which is the high spot of the entire visit, and not only because the central

The streets of the center are always clogged with traffic. At least once the visitor should take a spin in a carriage, the most classic and delightful means of transportation in the "red city".

The exterior of the two mausoleums which overlook a flourishing garden and contain the Saadian tombs. The main one is on the south, the second mausoleum on the north. Both date to the end of the sixteenth century, although they were "discovered" in 1917.

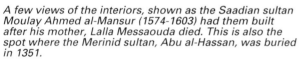

A few views of the interiors, shown as the Saadian sultan Moulay Ahmed al-Mansur (1574-1603) had them built after his mother, Lalla Messaouda died. This is also the spot where the Merinid sultan, Abu al-Hassan, was buried in 1351.

tomb is that of the Saadian Sultan, Moulay Ahmed al-Mansur. It is also the largest of the rooms (circa 10 mt. by 12), and is considered a true masterpiece of Hispano-Moresque art, with the formidable stalactite dome supported by twelve columns in Carrara marble. And then there are the polylobate arches, friezes with verses from the Koran, geometric motifs, painted and gilded cedarwood, majolica tiles and stuccoes. One feels as if one were inside an unbelievable piece of lace, further enriched by honeycomb intarsias. In addition to the tomb of al-Mansur, there are five other large ones and various smaller ones, of his children and grandchildren, which have triangular marble lids and are also embellished with other inscriptions.

A few details and a general view of the second room of the main mausoleum, on the south. This room, about 10 by 12 meters, is considered a masterpiece of Hispano-Moresque art. It is also known as the room of the 12 columns, all in Carrara marble. In addition to the remains of Moulay Ahmed al-Mansur (his tomb is the one in the center of the room) it contains five other large tombs and various burials of children and grandchildren. The polylobate arches, the friezes with verses from the Koran, the geometric patterns, the painted wood and the maiolica are also of particular note.

The third room, also called that of the three niches, contains only the tombs of children.

The second mausoleum, on the north, is not as important, and encloses the tomb of Lalla Messaouda. It is a square central plan structure of 4 x 4 meters, enclosed in a larger room, flanked by two loggias, all covered with a characteristic roof of green tiles. The niche containing the tomb of the mother of al-Mansur is completely decorated in honeycomb work. The garden, which stretches between the two mausoleums, helps make this site of memories and silence so highly and unforgettably evocative.

AL-BADI PALACE

This was undoubtedly the jewel of the "Saadian renaissance", although now only ruins remain of what was once a great palace. It was built by the indefatigable Ahmed al-Mansur, the most famous of the Saadian sultans, nicknamed "the golden one" for his boundless wealth, who had set himself the task of bringing back the splendor of a captital to the "red city".

On the other hand, before the advent of the Saadians Marrakesh had had its years of crisis marked by tribal clashes, under Merinid rule, when the capital was shifted to Fez. It was only with the arrival of the Saadians in the sixteenth century that Marrakesh once more flowered. The al-Badi palace must surely have been one of the marvels of this new life and glittering splendor. Ahmed al-Mansur began the great undertaking towards the end of 1578, right after the defeat he had inflicted on the Portuguese in the battle "of the three kings". Work is said to have lasted for 25 long years, up to the death of al-Mansur in 1603. The architect remains unknown, but it is certain that workers, architects, craftsmen and artists were called to the court of the Saadian sultan not only from the Maghreb, but also from Europe, Italy, Florence. The French writer Montaigne even wrote about the Carrara marble used for the columns. In the "Travel diary" he kept during his trip to France, Germany and Italy in 1580-1581, he noted that he had seen near Pisa various workers who were cutting and shipping marble "for a king of Morocco". And even more curious is the fact that all that marble seems to have been paid for in its weight in sugar. But in addition to the marble there must have been other treasures in the al-Badi palace: onyx, mosaics, stuccoes and ceilings in fine woods, one of the most complete inventories of Arab art including Andalusian influences. And then the gold, ceramics, doors of all kinds. Moulay Ismail plundered the palace treasures, and transferred much to Meknès, the city he had chosen as capital in place of Marrakesh which with his advent had once more fallen into disgrace. But it is also said that no city in the Maghreb was without something that had come from al-Badi.

Nothing of this palace, known as "the incomparable", now exists except for a few portions of

A fascinating view of the exterior of the al-Badi palace, the "jewel of the Saadian renaissance", of which only ruins remain after its destruction in 1696 by the Alaouite Sultan Moulay Ismail.

Another view of the al-Badi palace mirrored in the large inner pool. The Italian marble with which it was constructed was paid for by its weight in sugar.

A few views of the al-Badi palace. Nothing remains of its splendors but a few parts of the outer walls, the southwest and the northern pavilions.

exterior walls, the southwest and the north pavilions. The storks which leave every year on July 17th to the day perch on its walls. And beginning in 1961, the famous Festival of Folk Arts has been held here at the beginning of June every year. An event that encompasses folklore, music and dance, its fame has by now gone beyond the borders of Morocco and it has become a famous date on the entire international calendar of events.

The palace was built around a great rectangular court, with fine pools. Some ceramics can still be seen in what remains of the north pavilion, just after the entrance. There is also the access to the terrace from which one of the finest views of the entire city can be had. The old minbar, a sort of pulpit carved in wood, from the Koutoubia is to be seen in the pavilion towards the southwest.

A truly extraordinary feature. Every July 17th, to the day, the storks take off towards farther skies from the ruins of the al-Badi palace.

Ever since 1961 the famous Festival of Folk Arts, with music and dances by scores of folklore groups, is held here in the midst of this haunting setting of the crumbling walls of the al-Badi palace in early June.

BAHIA PALACE

There is good reason why the Bahia palace, undoubtedly one of the loveliest and richest to be found in Marrakesh, is known as "the resplendent". The entrance is on the corner of Rue Riad ez Zitoun el Jadid. It was expressly built towards the end of the nineteenth century to the requirements of Ba Ahmed, son of Si Moussa, grand vizier of Sidi Mohammed ben Abd er-Rahman and himself a vizier of the sultans Moulay Abd al-Aziz and Abd er-Rahman. Almost all on the ground floor, with a single apartment, the menzeh, on the first floor, it stretches out for around 8 hectares and is surrounded by splendid perfumed gardens.

The garden to the east of the palace is in the shape of a large trapezoid, 400 meters per side, with plants that are irrigated by the waters of a pool measuring 80 x 80 meters.

The architect El Haj Mohammed el Mekki employed seven years in its building (1894 to 1900), apparently counseled by a French officer, Erkmann. Row after row of apartments and rooms, richly decorated, seem to be laid out in an illogical ground plan. But this was in line with what Ba Ahmed desired. He refused to build other floors, except for the single apartment on the first floor, perhaps on account of his own stature and short legs, but kept on adding new rooms, never satisfied with what he had created. In his need for more space he bought many of the surrounding houses, and had

The interior court of the Bahia palace, the "resplendent". Built at the end of the nineteenth century, and almost all on a single level, it stretches out over 8 hectares and is surrounded by splendid gardens.

A few views of the rooms. It took the architect, el Haj Mohammed el Mekki, seven years (from 1894 to 1900) to build the Bahia.

Many references to Andalusian culture can be noted inside the palace with its wealth of decoration, but above all a cascade of Tetouan majolica tiles. Above and left: two views of the Council Hall.

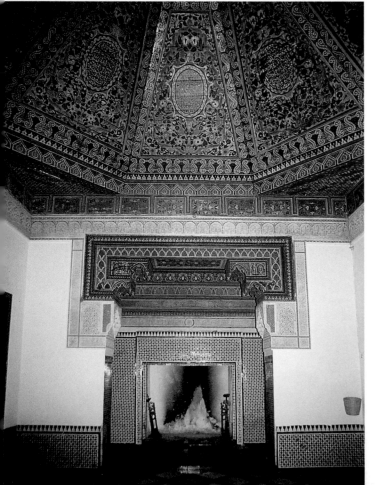

them torn down to enlarge his Bahia even further. Many of the apartments which make up this large complex bear witness to the preference of the architect for Andalusian culture and open on flowering gardens, with jasmine, oranges, cypresses. The rooms of the favorite or the spacious council hall, with its wealth of decorations and objects, can be admired, before going on to the rectangular room of honor, measuring 20 x 8 meters, with marble from Meknès in the floor. The ceilings are in intarsia cedarwood. But it is above all in the varicolored cascade of majolicas from Tetouan, the city founded in 1307 by the Merinid Sultan Abou Tabit, which became a corsair cove, where the Andalusian spirit clearly emerges in the colors and designs of the tiles.

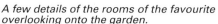

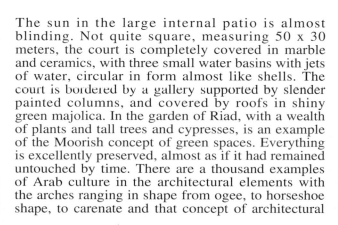

A few details of the rooms of the favourite overlooking onto the garden.

The sun in the large internal patio is almost blinding. Not quite square, measuring 50 x 30 meters, the court is completely covered in marble and ceramics, with three small water basins with jets of water, circular in form almost like shells. The court is bordered by a gallery supported by slender painted columns, and covered by roofs in shiny green majolica. In the garden of Riad, with a wealth of plants and tall trees and cypresses, is an example of the Moorish concept of green spaces. Everything is excellently preserved, almost as if it had remained untouched by time. There are a thousand examples of Arab culture in the architectural elements with the arches ranging in shape from ogee, to horseshoe shape, to carenate and that concept of architectural

beauty whose roots are to be found in the decorative function, entrusted to the facing, as well as to the geometry of the lines, the harmony of the colors, and the accessories. And it was here, in this palace which is half a city, that Ba Ahmed died on May 17 1900, to be buried in the Alaouite cemetery.

A splendid door inside the Bahia palace, with a doorway in cedar wood, aromatic and finely inlaid.

Other views of the palace. The sun can be blinding in the large square inner court, measuring 50 by 30 meters, and completely faced with marble and ceramics.

Top right: the mosque of the palace.

A view of the gardens, with a wealth of plants including tall trees, classical example of the Moorish concept of green spaces.

A few rich decoration with geometric and floral motifs.
Page 39: the prayer niche.

Below: details of the ceramic and majolica decoration and the "lacework" in repoussé stucco and carved wood.

A few aspects of the Governor's sleeping-room. Bottom right: the adjoining room. Almost everywhere the state of conservation is perfect.

A large polychrome ceramic decoration in the Bahia palace, with a predominance of floral over geometric motifs.

THE ROYAL PALACE

It is a pity that the royal palace is not open to the public. Only the external walls can be admired as they become almost bright red before sunset, that time of day when the sunlight is warmest in tone. The walls continue to join it to the great gardens of the Agdal, among the loveliest in Marrakesh, created in the twelfth century by the Almohad sovereign, Abd al-Mumin, and subsequently enlarged by the Saadians, famous above all for the olive trees.

The main aspect of the royal palace that can be enjoyed is the main entrance, with a shed roof above it in masonry, covered in green majolica tiles, in great contrast with the red of the walls.

The door is in the shape of a broken arch, surmounted by a sort of cornice in carved wood and covered by the later shed roof of green tiles. The arch is enriched by geometric motifs in a decoration of white and gilded relief stuccoes, which rest on a

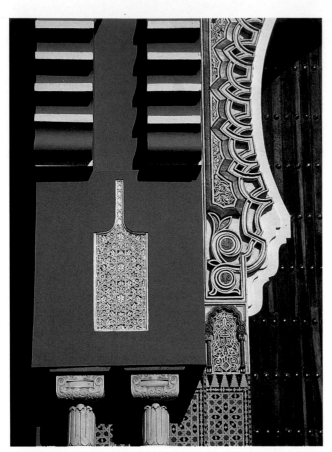

Detail of the decorations on the main entrance.

The main entrance of the royal palace, with the four small decorative columns at the sides, the wooden "ceiling" and the roof in green majolica.

The red walls and the main doorway of the Royal palace.

The interior and the door of the méchouar .

Facing page, above: the gate across which one enters the area in front of the royal palace, also known as "grand méchouar"; below: the pavilion of the Agdal gardens outside the méchouar.

base covered with majolicas with geometric ornamental motifs. On either side the door, almost acting as base and making the entire structure seem more slender, are two slim columns in white marble. The royal palace is almost opposite the al-Badi palace and near the Saadian tombs, in the southernmost part of the medina. To all extents it consists of the Ksar el Akhdar, the green palace, the garden which bears the name of the Nile, the magic river of the Egypt of the pharaohs and the Dar al Kubra, the great dwelling house.

The ancient palace of the sultan, Dar el-Makhzen was built by the Almohads and subsequently enlarged by the Saadians and was once one of the finest buildings in the city. Great basins of water were in the inner courtyards and one of these, it is said, was 500 "elbows" long.

BEN YOUSSEF MEDRASSA

In the heart of the historic medina, and a few steps from the fountain Chrob ou Chouf (drink and admire), waiting to be discovered are the Ben Youssef mosque, the Koubba al Baadiyin and the Ben Youssef Medrassa.

The mosque which was originally built by the Almoravids, was subsequently embellished by the Almohad Ali III, rebuilt anew in the sixteenth century, and further transformed in the nineteenth.

What is to be seen today therefore has nothing to do with the original building, of which only the koubba remains.

Only Muslims are allowed to enter this mosque, so that all we can do is look at the fine minaret with its roof of glazed green tiles, over 40 meters high, from the outside. As mentioned above, nothing remains of the original mosque but the Koubba al Baadiyin. This small annex, set lower in the ground, almost sunk in relation to the adjacent structures was not cleared and made visible until 1948.

Entrance and three views of the Ben Youssef Medrassa

But the most interesting objective is the IbnYusuf Medrassa. There is also another outstanding medrassa in Marrakesh, the one founded by the Alaouite Sultan Moulay er Rechid in the seventeenth century, but there is no doubt that this is by far the most important.

First of all a few words must be said on the importance of medrassas, actual schools of Koran theology, in the history of Morocco. Students who intended to pursue studies in the fields of religion, rhetoric, law, were housed here. But everything that was taught had been approved by the sultan beforehand and was in line with the untouchable canons of Islam. Upon leaving the medrassa the student might undertake a career in politics, devote himself completely to religion, or become a man of law. These colleges were always built near a mosque and were the fruit of the munificence of some sovereign. Inside, the rooms were laid out on a pre-established plan so that all medrassas have the same basic layout with all the rooms in the complex opening off a central court. The one in Marrakesh is the largest medrassa in all of Morocco. It was founded, in the middle of the fifteenth century, by the Merinid sultan Abu al-Hassan. In 1565 the works of renovation ordered in Saadian times by Moulay Abdallah were finished, as confirmed by the inscriptions in the prayer room. A long corridor, with a wealth of ornaments, is crossed upon entering. At each end is a marble basin for ablutions. The ornaments of the basin, made in Spain at the end of the tenth century, have floral motifs with birds. The small room next encountered serves as passage to the central court. There is something spell-binding in this fascinating court with a rectangular basin at the center and two galleries supported by columns running around it. The decorations range from marble and stucco, to the carved wood of the architraves, and the dominant pink tones lend the whole area an air of calm and serenity. Across the court, opposite the entrance from which we came, is the entry to the prayer room, covered by a dome in cedarwood, pierced by small windows and divided into three by slender columns. There is also a mihrab decorated with verses from the Koran. The rooms for the students can be seen the first floor. Those which overlook the central court are more spacious and lovelier than the more modest ones which open onto six secondary courts. All in all there are about a hundred small rooms, where the students withdrew at the end of their lessons and where they led a sober life without pomp or luxury.

Facing page, above: the prayer room and the study area with the prayer niche in the background.

Below: details of the decoration on a door and on the walls.

This page: the rooms for the students on the first floor.

PLACE DJEMAA EL-FNA

Djemaa el-Fna is much more than a square. It is a myth to see, experience, listen to, smell. All by itself it is one of the "places to go", a capital within a capital, unrivalled in fame and charm by any other square, European or American, or any other of those magical places where, at least once in a lifetime, one must say "I've been there".

But more than a square, it can be thought of as an ocean, as an enormous stage measuring 150 by 100 meters, between the medina and the Koutoubia which rises up to the sky, where the show changes from morning, afternoon, to night, a concentration of what Marrakesh is, its peoples of yesterday, in Berber and Arab costumes, women with their features hidden under veils and the men with their long heavy or light greatcoats, and the people of today in European dress with girls casually wandering around in skirts. Place Djemaa el-Fna is always open. No hours to be respected. Any time of day is the right time to go. It has always been the heart of life in the city. Yet it was also the place of death known as the "rendezvous of the dead" for it was here that the criminals sentenced to death by the sultan were once executed. There are at least three different squares to be seen, the morning square, the afternoon square and the evening square. In the morning Djemaa el-Fna is a great market place. It begins to fill with life even before the muezzin call

for prayer heralding the dawn. Slowly, apparently haphazardly, in an ever growing confusion which however has its almost ritual order, the stalls begin to come alive, colored umbrellas flower everywhere, and the merchants arrive. A cascade of fruit and vegetables appear wherever space is available: dates, oranges, bananas, apricots, peaches, plums, onions, watermelons, tomatoes, potatoes, lemons tangerines, grapefruit. The grocery stalls become extraordinary palettes. Pyramids of lentils, dry peas, chick peas, broad beans, beans, hide the faces of the venders, perched in the midst of their wares. Everything can be found in the market square. Spices: pepper, saffron, cinnamon, juniper, cumin, nutmeg, powdered chili peppers. And mountains of tea, above all imported from China, and cascades of green mint leaves. At a certain point all you can do is close your eyes and "look" with your nose. "Look" and dream, while a thousand fragrances waft through the air, from the essences which, together with henna (used by women to dye their hair and chosen by Mohammed as the symbol of peace), are on display in tiny mysterious colored bottles.

But the "grande place" is also an enticing foretaste of all the crafts you will find as you adventure further into the world of the souk (on foot naturally, there's no other way) whose lanes open out onto the immense market ocean, from every corner.

Two pictures of Place Djemaa el-Fna at two different times of day. There are at least "three" squares: the morning square, the afternoon square, and the evening square. The heart of the present and of the past of the old capital of southern Morocco beats here in this "rendezvouz of the dead". It is an enormous open-air stage, 150 by 100 meters, where everything can be found.

The great square begins to take on life when the first light of dawn fills the sky. This is when the first stands, with fruit and vegetables of all kinds, arrive. But the products of Moroccan crafts, leather, copper, soft pointed shoes, are also offered. And all around the air is full of all imaginable aromas and flavors.

Here are the famous "marocchinerie", objects in leather, bags, belts, of all kinds and styles; the soft babouches (slippers); plates and vases in ceramics and terra cotta; the daggers (and, with a bit of luck because they are becoming ever harder to find, the famous long-barrelled rifles of the "fantasias", engraved and encrusted like precious objects, one of the city's great old traditions); small tables with the top in brass or repoussè copper and fabrics, textiles, yarns. There's no way of leaving without at least being tempted to buy a jellaba, the cloth shirt both men and women wear; the serual or "knickers"; a fine red fez to set on top of one's head; the hanbel or cloak of dark wool used by the Berber women of the High Atlas, caftans from the simpler kind to the more precious ones decorated and embroidered in gold and silver.

And about halfway through the afternoon, almost unawares, you'll find that Place Djemaa el-Fna has been transformed into an enormous stage for a show that is taking place everywhere. No tickets to buy but, since you are tourists, you might offer a few coins. But nobody will pester you; nobody will attach themselves to you. And these are the thousand personages who will pass before your eyes, all you have to do is look around, move from one corner to the other of this enormous state where everything takes place on the ground, on, or off, large and small carpets. Here is a snake charmer. A musician next to him playing shrill notes on his flute and the charmer, after uncovering his basket, plays with his snake, lightly and skilfully taps his head, grasps his body at just the right point with swift gestures. Snake charmers are part of a myth, an ancient legacy, perhaps of a sacred tradition that came here from far-off India.

A tourist show? Perhaps, but not only. And have fun watching the fire eaters; the musicians beating their gembrit, the drums, in an incessant rhythm; the Gnawa dancers, of Sudanese origin, black as coal and agile as gazelles. Admire the water venders, and why not, buy a cupful. Together with mint tea, the water of the venders can stand as a symbol of the liquid soul of Marrakesh. With their red garments, white shirts, those big hats with cloth ropes dangling from the edge and the shiny copper or brass cups, ready to be used, the water venders are one of the indelible emblems of Marrakesh, of Morocco, but also of the Arab world. Their costumes may differ but they are the same venders who wander through the streets of Istanbul, through the streets of the entire Arab world, where water,

never enough, is as sacred as life, is the most precious of wares, the simplest but also the richest offering anyone can make and which in any case will be made in every house, rich or poor, where you enter.

Don't miss the chance to take a good look at this world with its magicians and fortune tellers, its monkey trainers. Stop for a minute on the terrace of the cafè de France, one of the many locales which stand at the edge of this "sea", together with other shops and small restaurants. You can take it all in in a single glance: the square and its actors; the green gardens which break up the red of Marrakesh; the Gueliz, the city of today with the geometric forms and spaces of a modern metropolis; the mountains of the High Atlas, their peaks, such as the Toubkal (4165 m.), the highest peak in northern Africa, gleaming white with snow in winter.

But it is at night that Place Djemaa el-Fna turns into the most fabulous of fables. The acetylene lamps are lighted, above all on the ground where the exhibitions and dances continue and where people sit in circles, sipping the mythical mint tea. Hundreds of "bare" light bulbs, connected to simple electric wires, form glowing canopies over the booths and shops.

Snake charmers, perhaps the most famous attraction of the great show in Place Djemaa el-Fna.

A typical stand where the vender offers his wares. There are hundreds and hundreds and each one sets up business wherever there is room, beginning his litany of appeals, gestures, glances, trying to inveigle the customer into buying.

Discussion and bargaining are an essential element in the Arab culture so be prepared to haggle over the price.

Three water venders, in their typical costumes.

The aromas and flavors of food fill the air. This, rather than at lunch, is the time when it pays to sit at a stand on wheels, or under the shed roof of a small restaurant and try at least one of the specialties of Moroccan cuisine. An infinity of choices includes spits of roasted mutton; kefta meat balls made with parsley, onion and chili peppers; the fantastic briouat, a sort of salted flaky pastry, cylindrical, rectangular, full of ground meat and spices in a hundred different ways; the bstila, a salty pie of sheets of pastry filled with

Night is pure magic in Place Djemaa el-Fna, illuminated by a myriad of acetylene lamps.

pigeon, almonds, cinnamon, saffron and eggs; the touajen, superb stews where the meat is first fried and can be either mutton or beef, and at times fish, and is then mixed with dates, varied vegetables and, obviously, spices. Don't worry, lay your fears aside. You'll be surprised to see how well sweet and salt go together in unexpected ways. And don't leave the square until you have tasted a slice of honey cake, a handful of roasted dates, a piece of griouch, once more honey and sesame seeds together.

DAR SI SAID MUSEUM

The visit to the ethnological museum of Dar Si Said, not far from the Bahia palace, is a must. Completely renovated in 1978 by the government and still growing as new and interesting objects continue to be added (as in the case of the ceramics room), Dar Si Said is a museum in more than one way.

First because of what it contains and secondly because the premises themselves are an outstanding piece of architecture.

The palace dates to the end of the nineteenth century, and was built by the vizier of Moulay Abd al-Aziz, Ba Ahmed and finished by his brother, Si Said. Considered one of the loveliest palaces in the city, it became the official residence in 1914 and was subsequently transformed into a museum in 1932.

Its rooms house objects, ornaments, weapons, carpets, which narrate the story of Marrakesh, but also that of the entire south of Morocco. It is truly unique. To the right upon entering is a "map" with the explanation and localization of the rooms. The gates of the southern casbah covered with geometric decoration, whose meaning has still to be interpreted by scholars, are visible as one passes into a vaulted corridor.

To be noted are two outstanding swings in wood, with an explanation of how they worked. And it is in the patio with its garden that you can breathe the atmosphere of these rooms, surrounded by orange and date trees, by palms which perfume the air and a central pool, hexagonal in marble.

The actual museum runs around the garden, on which the four rooms on the ground floor open. The jewel room on the south contains an exhibition which bears witness to the different forms, the

Dar Si Said Museum: two aspects of the rooms on the ground floor.

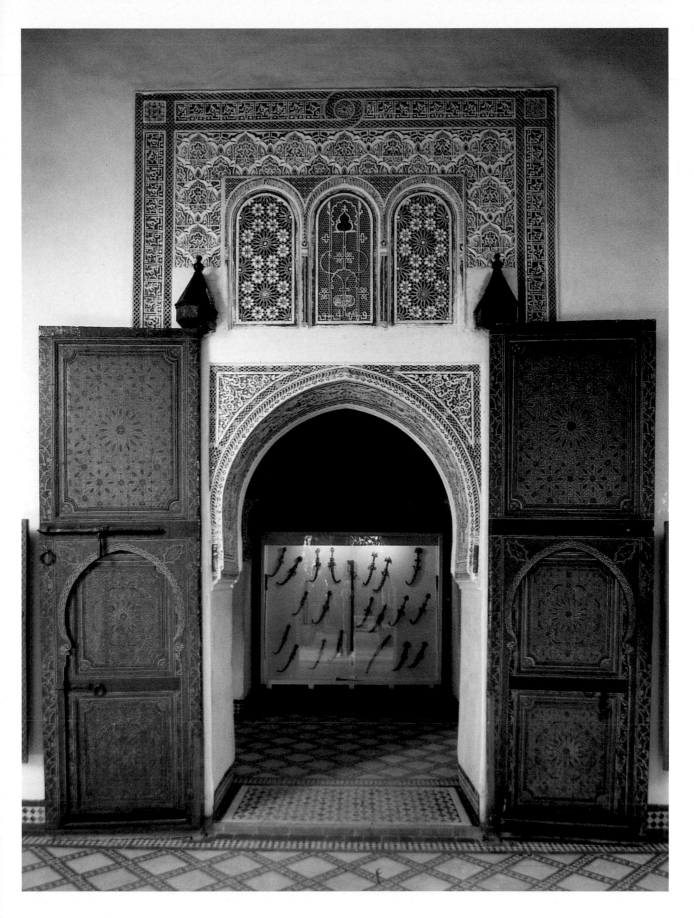

Another view of the ground floor.

techniques, including the oldest ones, used by the Berber and Arab peoples to create frontals, diadems, southern crosses, filigree, engraved fibulas. Finely embroidered wedding caftans are included among the examples on exhibition in the caftan room. The room of the coppers and brasses furnishes evidence of one of the most typical craft activies of Morocco, with trays and ewers in brass or red copper from the region of Igherm. In the weapon room, if you have seen a "fantasia" at least once, you will recognize the long rifles used in the charges, the powder flasks, but also splendid examples of other types of weapons, (sabers, daggers).

The museum continues on the first floor. At the top of the steps is a square room with blue and white mosaics on the floor and walls. Hispano-Moresque influence is obvious here, as in other buildings in the city, in the designs, the colors, the geometrical patterns. The square room also contains Rabat carpets, old and authentic, and chairs of perfumed wood, used in wedding ceremonies. The adjacent room contains Tensift carpets, and other pieces typical of the High Atlas and the Berber tradition. Still to be seen is a smaller court where wooden panelling dating from the sixteenth century (Saadian period), and saved from the al-Badi palace, is on view. Before leaving, be sure to take a look at the black mantles, bordered with orange-red motifs, known as Akhnif, and used by the Ait Ouaouzguit Berber shepherds.

THE SOUK

A tour through the souk has to begin in Place Djemaael-Fna, to continue on either Rue des Potiers or Rue des Epiciers. Depending on which one you take, you encounter the first souk of the potters, or a small market of vegetables and candied fruit side by side with a few butcher stands where the heads and innards of sheep are sold.

But the real entrance to the magic of the souk quarter is through a large white gate which opens onto the Semmarin souk, in the street of the same name, full of cloth venders. Here we are then where the heart of the city beats strongest, in the midst of a river of people walking, suddenly stopping, talking, shouting, gesticulating. It is easy to get lost, but it is never anything to worry about. Everything that the crafts of Marrakesh has to offer the tourist can be found here, as well as merchandise and objects of daily life for the inhabitants of the city. Over 10,000 craftsmen have organized into 40 corporations and every type of merchandise or craft work, or almost, has its own particular souk: from that of the leather workers, to that of the dyers, the coppersmiths, the iron smiths, the goldsmiths, the babouche makers. Buying something, after having looked and compared unhurriedly, between one cup of mint tea

and another which is often offered, certainly means bargaining, but it is a custom one should respect. Continuing on the same road one reaches the Rahba Kedima, a small square, which in the past was a market for slaves and grain, and which now contains a fruit and vegetable market. In the environs of this small square are the wool souk and the sheepskin souk. In the northernmost part of the square, and it is easy to find with its cascade of colors, is the carpet souk. It is known as Zarbia, the Berber auction. Finding one's way through the lanes, you can return to a larger road, Souk el-Kebir, and then the jewellery market and slip into the oldest part of the entire district, the Kissaria, the corridors. After going through various noteworthy gates, you find yourself in a labyrinth of slanting passageways, all covered with wood and where the sun, filtering from a few openings in the roof, creates picturesque violent contrasts of light and shade. This is where the realm of the leather workers begins, venders of jackets and coats of all styles, piled up one on top of the other, hanging over your head, almost brushing your hair, often forcing you to duck down. Outside, back on the Rue du Souk el-Kebir, other leather craftsmen offer belts, hats, bags of all sizes. The tour continues up to the Cherratine souk. And from here we begin

A view of the medina.

Two streets in the souk, the markets, the great city of shops, where over 10,000 artisans, belonging to forty different corporations, live and work day and night.

our way back, but through other souk, which at the end take us back to Place Djemaa el-Fna.

Not far from the Cherratine souk, after passing the Ibn Yusuf mosque and turning into Rue Baroudienne and Rue Amesfah, and after casting a glance at the lovely Chrob ou Chouf (drink and admire) fountain, we can detour to the Sidi bel Abbas mosque. The adjacent mausoleum houses the tomb of Sidi bel Abbas, who lived in Marrakesh during the reign of Yakub el-Mansur to teach in the medina, and who is one of the seven patrons of the city. Their tombs are still today objects of veneration and are scattered throughout the historical medina (Sidi Yusuf, who became leprous; Cadi Ayad, magistrate in Granada and in Ceuta for the Almoravids; Sidi ben Slimane, who proclaimed himself descendent of Mohammed; Sidi Abd el-Aziz, famous scientist; Sidi el-Ghezouani, who was also imprisoned and Sidi Essoheyli, the author of famous works).

Continuing our round from where we were, in the Smata souk we will overwhelmed by the famous babouches. There are thousands of them and they are hung up everywhere, forming the very walls of these small unique little shops. Embroidered with gold thread, sometimes with curving points, sometimes simpler, for many the babouches are an irresistible attraction. This is one of the most characteristic and delightful places. Continuing further is the phantasmagoria of the colors of the dyers' souk. Here the lanes of the district have been transformed into drying racks with red, yellow, green, brightly colored skeins of wool and silk hung out in the sun on canes or long wooden poles from one side of the lane to the other, making a roof over your heads. But it is also interesting to watch the craftsmen at work, as well as looking at their wares. Busy around large cauldrons they are preparing the dye baths in the greatest variety of hues which were once all natural but now use chemical products. A lane goes down hill to the Mouassin mosque and fountain. But if we move off into the Rue du Souk Attarine, towards the left, leaving the dyers behind, we reach the souk of the smiths and across from it that of the coppersmiths. The first thing that strikes one here is the never-ending sound of small and large hammers. The work in wrought iron reveals strong Spanish influences as a result of the contacts of the great Almoravid, Almohad, Saadian and Merinid dynasties had with Spain and is true engraver's art. On the other hand Marrakesh is full of windows with wrought iron grates and Arabesqued gates. The copper workers are also highly skilled, hammering out great repoussè plates, brass pitchers, lamps in many different shapes. The tour of the souk quarter comes to an end with a final glance at the countless porters bent double under enormous weights, always asking that one make way. Place Djemaa el-Fna and its open spaces are there waiting for us.

Two different shop interiors in the souk. Everything can be found: carpets, textiles, silks, soft leather slippers and bags. It is all on view in such an incredible abundance that the walls of the shops are completely covered.

CARPET SOUK

A folk legend says that it was a stork who gave the women of Morocco the chance to learn this ancient art by letting a piece of carpet from Asia Minor fall into the courtyard of a Moroccan house. In the Zarbia souk we can find carpets of every type and color, each part of the original tradition of this or that city in Morocco. The Rabat carpets, among the best known, generally use seven colors and are full of magical designs. The Chichaua, with a red, pink or black ground and asymmetrical patterns, come from the Haouaz plain, but are not made in Marrakesh. The Glaous are very fine. Hues ranging from red to blue characterize the Ait Ouaouzguite, named after the High Atlas tribe which weaves them. The Berber carpets are recognizable because they are usually of long wool yarns with the ends knotted and a preference for red, obtained from madder root. The use of diamond shaped geometrical motifs in a variety of colors comes from the High Atlas. Other well known types of carpets are the Zemmour, the Beni Ouarain, the Zain, the Marmoucha.
Various types of looms, both vertical and horizontal, can be observed in the souk as well as work in progress, if one is lucky.

LEATHER WORKERS SOUK

To be found mostly in the kissaria, the open corridors in the old heart of the market quarter, the first thing that strikes the visitor is the smell of leather. In working leather, the Moroccans have become famous abroad and the "art of the marocchinerie", with its capital in Fez, is the pride of the nation. Of particular note is goat leather, called Flali, for in the past it came from the city of Tafilalet. If you have time to wait just a few minutes, you can see how quickly these craftsmen can make a pillow case or the typical sukara, the bags men wear like bandoleers, originally from the Rif. The secret of this leather also lies in how the skins are tanned. This is done in the area east of the medina, near Bab Debbagh, the tanners' gate, which overlooks the quarter of the same name. Despite the "aroma", it is something that must be seen. In spacious or narrow courtyards between the houses, the men are at work, their feet in the large round or rectangular tubs where the skins are washed, scraped, softened, before being set into the sun to dry. Hard work which also includes dying the skins, immersed in dye baths just as was done centuries ago, in the times of the Almoravids, the founders of the city.

Two pictures of the carpet souk, full of color and intense contrasts. All kinds of carpets can be found here: Rabat, from the Haouaz plain, from the High Atlas, or from the Chichaua and the Glaous.

 MOROCCAN CRAFTS

Dipping into their ancient history, the producer of an oral (Berber) and written (Arab) art and culture, always hoarding up the experiences of the past, of the encounters or clashes with other peoples and other civilizations (Carthaginians, Roman, Vandals, Byzantines, and afterwards, from 682 on, the Arabs), the Moroccans have created one of the richest and most varied craft traditions known today.

Indeed the production in this field is one of the most important economic activities in Morocco today, above all in Fez, Meknès, and even more so in Marrakesh, the three indisputable capitals. But the same can be said for the smaller towns such as Essaouira, on the Atlantic between Agadir and Safi, famous for the working of tuia wood, lemon and ebony.

According to the most recent surveys, over 58% of the population of Marrakesh makes its living on crafts. A well ordered world, organized into corporations or guilds (there are 40 in the city of the Koutoubia) under the control of the Mohtaseb, who watches over the management of the Amin, the heads of the individual corporations.

As we can see, souks and medinas are the beating heart of a many-faceted activity. Gold and silver, copper and brass, leather and wood are worked. Carpets and textiles, in silk and wool, are woven. Pottery of all kinds and uses is made. Musical instruments and weapons, objects for the house, containers of all types are made. And all this in a society such as that of Morocco, certainly projected towards a future with an even more intense industrial development, but also with an economical present that still rests firmly on the craft activities, on the skill of the hands of these fine engravers, workers in repoussè, decorators, tailors, leather workers.

The great boom in tourism in the past years has also opened new spaces, new markets for the crafts, at the same time permitting older traditions that were almost headed for extinction (for example the manufacture, in Marrakesh itself, of the famous rifles, the moukkala, for the "fantasias") to survive.

This skill and this creativity, to be found in every truly Moroccan object (and by this we mean that here too the markets, sometimes, have also become, in part at least, centers of a "plastic geography" to be found at all latitudes), derives directly from the canons of beauty and the concepts that are part of the Arab world. According to these canons the human figure must not be depicted, cannot be shown for religious reasons as well. And this is why all the attention and all their skill is concentrated on the external aspect, on "describing" everything outside the human spirit, as Alhazen, a great philosopher who lived in the 10th century, preached and wrote with regards to beauty. This is why everything that expresses the taste for decoration through the patterns is beautiful; the repetition of

The streets that lead to the souk.

Objects of Moroccan crafts and jewelry of Berber tradition, with silver bracelets, brooches, pendants with semi-precious stones and corals and rings of all kinds which were ordered from the master craftsman (the mahalem).

signs, such as the Arab script itself, which we find in the thousand inscriptions in the mosques; or the repetition of the geometric strokes in a great variety of colors on the tiles and glazed ceramics.

It might be well to make a list of at least some of these extraordinary handmade objects: the choukaras, finely worked leather articles; wrought iron, from grates to gates, to lamps; daggers with intarsia handles and rifles with long barrels; jewellery in silver from the south such as brooches, bracelets, pendants with semi precious stones and corals, the rings which were ordered from the master craftsman (the mahalem) when the harvest went well; the hand knotted carpets, some with over a hundred thousand knots per square meter; objects in hammered copper, the specialty of Taroudant, and in engraved copper from Marrakesh; the terra cottas with the major center in Fez; the innumerable utensils in wood.

CRAFTS IN WOOD

The working of wood is one of the oldest traditions. The many inlaid ceilings of the great palaces of Marrakesh, the decorations of balconies and cornices, some of the splendid mihrabs, the pulpits of the mosques facing Mecca, all bear witness to its age. A whole series of objects in wood can be found in the medina, near the Chouari souk: dishes, stools for large brass trays, sculptured objects which look like openwork lace. And that the art of wood is one of the oldest is also witnessed by the many large and small doors of the palaces scattered throughout the old city or the two doors saved from the al-Bahi palace and now on view in the ethnological museum of Dar Si Said. And then there are the chairs, chests of drawers, musical instruments, rifle stocks, bellows. All work done with sharp gauges and slender pointed knives. Cedar, tuia, lemon wood, ebony all submit to the hands of the craftsman. The inlaid boxes, which often almost look embroidered, so fine are the inlays, are true marvels. But it is not only sight that is satisfied in the woodworkers shop, for the intense penetrating perfume of the old and new aromatic woods is something we will not easily forget.

The working of wood, one of the oldest traditions.

WOOL SOUK

This is one of the first to be encountered in the long tour in the quarter of the souk. In a sense it overlooks Place Rahba el Kdima, where slaves and grain were once sold. The wool souk in part gives us a foretaste of the spectacle of colors, with skeins hung up and perfumes which will explode around us in the dyers souk, one of the last in our tour, which began in Place Djemaa el-Fna, just before the Mouassin fountain, where there is another gate of the great labyrinth of wares. The shops are full of skeins hung up everywhere. And the fringed white cloaks of the Berber women of the High Atlas, called hanbel, are in wool; as are the black mantles of the shepherds, called Akhnif. For, strange as it may seem, wool is essential in the fiery Sahara, for wool is what protects one from an implacable sun.

Three views of the wool souk which overlooks Place Rahba el Kdima. The souk is a riot of colors and perfumes, with skeins hung up to dry above our heads and cauldrons where the yarns are soaked.

A craftsman in front of his shop, as he patiently arranges mountains of many-colored yarns. This is what you will see if you raise your eyes in the lanes of the wool souk: in place of the sky....a cascade of colors.

OBJECTS FOR THE HOME, COPPER AND POTTERY

If you get the chance, don't miss visiting a house in Marrakesh. It is also a way to get a closer look at the objects of daily life.

The city house is not at all like the fortified dwellings protected by crenellation such as the ksur, the fortress-houses of the notables, or the tiguemmi, the dwellings in the villages, in beaten earth and stone, not to mention the tent-houses (in wool or dwarf palm fibre textile) of the duar, the shepherd camps.

It is impossible to get an idea of what the city house, like all Arab houses, looks like from the street, for they are all turned inwards, with no particular openings. The classical square structure always centers around an inner garden or small patio. The house is the absolute realm of the women, who when they enter as brides bring a lamb, the symbol of fertility.

The furniture inside may be inlaid, constructed of perfumed wood such as tuia, or it may be more simple, depending on the economic conditions of

The working of copper is also one of the oldest of Moroccan crafts. Hammered copper is a specialty of Taraoudant, engraved copper is typical of Marrakesh. There are all types and sizes of trays, ready to be set on the indispensable small folding wooden tables.

Spices, dates, dried fruit and aromas of all kinds are sold everywhere - along the street and on the "grande place", or in the more hidden shops of the medina.
Aromas are absolute rulers here: juniper, cinnamon, nutmeg, cumin, saffron. Without these essences, Marrakesh would not be the same.

Typical lanes of the medina.

the family. There are always stools, generally low and small, and the meida, very low tables, used for the diffa, the classic Moroccan meal. But it will not be easy to find tableware, for the Arabs prefer to eat "with three fingers". And we will find that shoes are outright dispensed with in the dining room. Eating without cutlery is a true art, almost impossible to master for those of us who have not learned it as children.

Lovely trays in brass or yellow or red copper hold the varied foods of the diffa, including couscous, the most famous of all. The most important plates are usually enamelled with the same five colors (blue, green, yellow, white and brown).

Hammered copper objects are the specialty of Taroudant, those in engraved copper of Marrakesh.

But first of all we will be offered perfumed orange water in which to wash our hands. In Moroccan houses earthenware is of great importance: terracotta pitchers and amphoras abound. Particularly lovely are the blue ones, typical of Fez,

The large typical open-air tubs where textiles and skins are dyed and where the air at times is absolutely unbreathable.

A typical courtyard surrounded by the craftsmen's shops.

Two views of the medina.

which is the capital, and whose origins are Hispano-Moresque. The vases, many with all kinds of lids, may or may not have geometrical decorations. Those most frequently found have designs of flowers and leaves. But the "set" will also include straw covered flasks, goblets, footed or non footed bowls. Extremely thin glasses are normally used for the mint tea and here too fantasy has been given free reign: bellied, small, larger and some with a gold rim.

A special place goes to the objects in straw and wicker, the simplest baskets, and others that are "zebra striped", with threads of colored straw.

Anyone who wants to buy objects of domestic use but who is not necessarily interested in going to the souk, could go to the Monday market of Ourika.

A pavilion in the Menara gardens.

A view of the large "pool" in the Menara gardens, almost a lake measuring 150 by 200 meters.

GARDENS OF MARRAKESH

 The splendor of Marrakesh could never have been had it not been for water. And this was what the Almoravids, founders of the city, immediately looked for, exploiting it to the last drop. It is from the waters of the Oued Tensift, which borders the Palmeraie and from the 350 wells connected by that unbelievable network of the khettara, the subterranean canals which still today are in working order, that the wealth arrived which permitted this city on the confines of the desert with its burning sands, to defeat thirst, to give birth to the most characteristic craft operations such as the working and tanning of leather, and the dying of fabrics, and of providing itself with splendid gardens, with a wealth of plants of all kinds, of great pools and

fountains such as those of Sidi el Hassan or Mouassin. The three great gardens of the Berber capital, which almost enclose it in an imaginary triangle from north to south and from south to west are the Menara, the Majorelle gardens and the Agdal.

 ## MENARA GARDENS

The Menara, to the west, is an ensemble of several gardens which covers an area measuring 1200 m. in length by 800 wide, protected by an enclosure in beaten earth 4 km. long. The great central pool is almost a lake of 150 by 200 m, realized as early as the twelfth century by the Almohads.

Pavilion in the Menara gardens, views of the interior and a view from the windows overlooking the pool.

The finishing touches were added by the Alaouites, who came after the Saadians, thanks above all to Sidi Mohammed ben Abd er Rahman, in the second half of the nineteenth century. The garden has above all a wealth of olive trees and near the central pond where the entire network of canals centers is a typical pavilion, of Saadian epoch, with a pyramidal roof covered with green glazed tiles, and with a sort of balcony which overlooks the surroundings. There is something spell-binding about this place, above all at sunset, when a thousand reflections are caught in the waters of the pool. Everywhere there is a great feeling of peace and space.

MAJORELLE GARDENS

To get to the Majorelle Gardens one takes Avenue Yacoub el-Mansour and then a small lane on the left. Their fame and charm are due in particular to the incredible number and variety of birds which live in the midst of the bougainvilleas, cypresses, bamboos and banana trees. There is also an important exhibition of cactus. Created by a famous French cabinet maker, Louis Majorelle (1859-1926), they has been somewhat neglected in the past, but are now once more as splendid as ever, with the addition of new curiosities, thanks to the famous stylist Yves Saint Laurent who bought them not so long ago. A museum of Islamic art, with carpets, household wares and objects of the classic Moroccan crafts has been installed in a pavilion of a deep blue color. A visit is practically a must.

Two views of the pavilions in the Majorelle gardens, created by a French cabinet-maker of great fame in the nineteenth century.

The Majorelle gardens are famous above all for the incredible number of birds of all species to be found there.

AGDAL GARDENS

The Agdal Gardens stretch out, on the south, beneath the great walls of the royal palace.

Of considerable size, they measure three by one and a half km. In addition to olives there are numerous fruit trees: oranges, tangerines, apricots, plums, pomegranates, apples and pears. It is an ideal place for long restful walks. This is what Moulay Abd er-Rahman (1822-1859) had in mind, when he surrounded them with an enclosing wall with a few towers. The gates now there were added by Moulay el-Hassan, a score of years later. The gardens are divided in two parts by a broad avenue which cuts through from south to north. Thre are two large pools. The first, al Gersifa, also has a small island; the second should be seen above all at sunset when an old and battered Saadian palace, Dar el Hana, is reflected in the water.

Two other views of the gardens.

Three views of the small but highly interesting museum of Islamic art, with carpets, household wares and craft objects. The museum was created by the famous stylist Yves Saint Laurent who bought the complex for just that purpose.

THE MODERN CITY

A river of continuous traffic runs along the great arteries which cut through the quarters of the modern city. The "red city", Marrakesh with its ancient walls and the narrow lanes of the souk, seems far away here where the broad streets of the Gueliz fan out. The life that runs frenetically through these broad streets, perfumed by jacaranda and orange trees, shaded by palms whose fronds wave gently or toss violently in the wind, is like that of any metropolis where tall modern buildings rise up one next to the other. But Marrakesh, with its international airport, and over 600,000 inhabitants (counting those of the neighboring dour, the closest suburbs), is also this. Avenue Mohammed V, the longest boulevard, joins three large squares, Place Abd el-Moumen ben Ali, Place du 16 Novembre, Place de la Liberté, and then peters out, towards the old heart, at the foot of the Koutoubia.

Public offices, banks and hotels are situated in a variety of modern buildings. The office windows of the principal airlines overlook spacious sidewalks,

Convention Center.

A panorama from above of the modern city. Instead of the souk and the lanes of the medina, modern streets and spacious avenues intersect each other here, in this city of over 600,000 inhabitants, projected towards the future as well as aware of its past.

as do those of the most fashionable shops. Marrakesh is both a capital of the past and of the present - of the Morocco of Hassan II. And the sovereign is particularly devoted to this ancient city, which is also trying to keep up with the times. The development of the new quarters began in the sixties and seventies and is still continuing. This is where many of the new deluxe hotels can be found, such as the Hotel Pullman, and facilities of all kinds (an example are the splendid golf courses which attract golfers from all over the world). And this is where the structures of the fine convention center rise up, a contemporary version in which older traditions have been blended with the new.

International tourism has discovered and turned this city into one of its favorite haunts. The years in which only the young people of Europe seemed to be drawn by the charm of this city full of atmosphere, sounds and perfumes, seem far off indeed. Today Marrakesh on an average has annually two tourists for each of its inhabitants and it is tourism which is vying seriously with the principal economic activity of once: that magic world of crafts, closed in the coffers of the thousand souk.

Another view of the Convention Center.

A modern tourist complex, respectful of the local building tradition.

HOTEL MAMOUNIA

Of the plethora of hotels to be found in Marrakesh nowadays, the Hotel Mamounia has a story all its own. A visit to admire the park or the decorations in the foyer and the dining room, or a glance from the terraces where the whole quarter of the casbah lies before your eyes as far as the peaks of the High Atlas, is a must.

Situated in Avenue Bab el Jedid, not far from the ancient walls of the city, it was designed in 1923 by the architects Prost and Marchisio and is set in the midst of the fine Mamounia Gardens which were originally created by the Saadians, and were then given to Prince el-Mamun, as a wedding present. With a wealth of orange and olive trees, under the French protectorate the gardens were then divided, and part was turned over to the nearby hospital. The hotel was renovated and restored at the end of the 1970s and now has almost 200 rooms, some of them super de luxe, including various suites (the royal apartments, or the Marocchini). Part of its fame and charm also depend on the fact that the great English statesman Winston Churchill chose it as the his headquarters when he came for long periods of repose and began writing his memoirs between one cigar and another, with an occasional walk in the green gardens, and a glance from the terrace.

Four views of the Hotel Mamounia. Built in 1923, it became famous when Winston Churchill began to come here for extended periods of vacation and meditation.

THE PALMERAIE

A legend says that the great palm grove, The Palmeraie, was created by the Almoravid soldiers of Yusuf ibn-Tashfin, the founder of Marrakesh. Encamped in the Haouz valley where the city would eventually rise, they threw the pits of the quantities of dates they ate on the ground and the result was The Palmeraie. The Palmeraie is situated in the area north of Marrakesh, and stretches up to the banks of the Oued Tensift, covering an area around 13,000 hectares. Today the grove, as luxuriant as ever, still leaves room for fruit trees, pomegranates, oranges and vegetable gardens. They'll tell you there are at least 150,000 plants in this large park, but who knows if they have really counted them. In any case none of this would have been possible without one of the best-known Almoravid creations: the kettara, the subterranean conduits which go from one to the other of the over 350 wells in the city and distribute the water. It was Ali, the son of Yusuf ibn-Tashfin, who entrusted their construction to an engineer, Abdallah ben Younes. The Palmeraie is an enormous green lung that separates the city from the outskirts. To get there, take the road to Casablanca and pass the hills of the Gueliz and the new city.

The modern tourist complex of The Palmeraie, one of the greatest available a few kilometers from Marrakesh, which also sports a splendid golf course.

OUZOUD FALLS

It is well worth while to take a trip to the Middle Atlas, 150 km. from Marrakesh, first along the P24 and then the road 1811. The Ouzoud Falls are the highest in all of North Africa, with a drop of 110 meters in a striking landscape.

The source of the Oum er-Rbia river is also to be found in the mountains of the Middle Atlas. The most important river in Morocco, it flows 600 km. before emptying into the Atlantic just north of El-Jadida. Among its affluents is the Oued el-Abid, of which the Ouzoud Falls are part.

Here, as in the imposing Victoria Falls, it is almost impossible not to have a glittering rainbow stand out against the blue sky. The fall of almost 110 meters takes the waters of the Oued Ouzoud, a typically unstable Morrocan mountain torrent, whose source is 3 km. further upstream, down to the canyon where the Oud el-Abid runs, a kilometer below.

The tourist boom of latter years has made it a favorite site for foreign visitors but also for the Moroccans themselves who love to come here when they have a holiday, stopping in one of the many cafes and small restaurants in the vicinity.

If you come by car, you can park in a spacious area and continue on foot to reach the falls.

The sight from below, with the noisy foaming waters falling from one rock to another, is truly striking.

A path flanked by olive trees leads to the base of the falls.

Climbing up the path you can look down over the edge of the cliff, taking in at a glance the waterfall below, the vegetation of the rocky walls with its thousand shades of green, of all intensities, and the distant horizon, with the peaks of Djebel Azourki (3900 m.) and Djebel Ghat (3825 m.).

The Ouzoud Falls, a spectacle of the power of Nature. Although they are located 150 kilometers from Marrakesh, it is worth while to make the detour. With a fall of 110 meters, they are the highest falls in northern Africa.

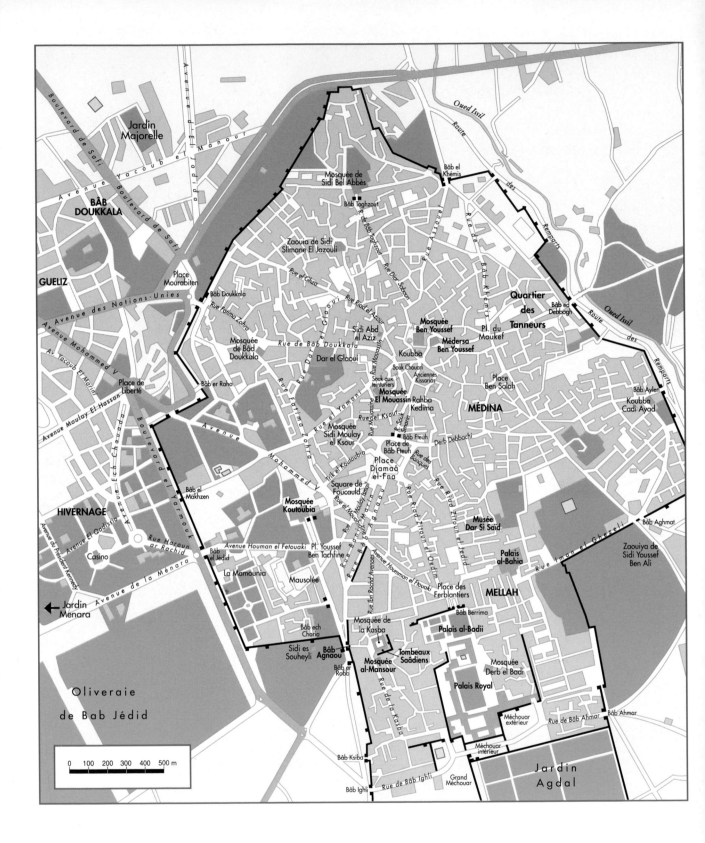

Jardin
Majorelle

Boulevard de Safi

Avenue Yacoub el Mansour

Oued Issil

Route des

**BÂB
DOUKKALA**

Avenue Boulevard de Safi

Mosquée de
Sidi Bel Abbès

Bâb el
Khémis

Zaouia de Sidi
Slimane El Jazouli

Bâb Taghzout

GUELIZ

Avenue des Nations-Unies

Place
Mourabiten

Bâb Doukkala

Rue de Bâb Taghzout

Rue Dar Dbachi

Rue Diar Saboun

**Quartier
des
Tanneurs**

Bâb el
Debbagh

Oued Issil

Avenue Mohammed V

Rue Fatima Zohra

Rue el Gza

Rue Riad el Arous

Rue de Bâb Khémis

Route des

Av. Yacoub El Marini

Mosquée
de Bâb
Doukkala

Rue de Bâb Doukkala

Sidi Abd
el Aziz

**Mosquée
Ben Youssef**

Pl. du
Moukef

Remparts

Avenue Moulay-El Hassan

Place de
Liberté

Bâb er Raha

Rue Dar el Glaoui

Dar el Glaoui

Koubba

**Médersa
Ben Youssef**

Bâb Aylen

Souk Chouari

Rue Mouassine

Place
Ben Salah

Koubba
Cadi Ayad

Rue Fatima Zohra

Rue Yamani

Souk aux
teinturiers

Anciennes
Kissarias

**Mosquée
El Mouassin**

Rahba
Kedima

MÉDINA

Rue de Bâb Doukkala

Rue el Ksour

Souk Smarin

Boulevard el Yarmouk

Bâb el
Makhzen

Rue Moulay el Ksour

Mosquée
Sidi Moulay
el Ksour

Bâb Fteuh

Derb Debbachi

HIVERNAGE

Avenue

Mohammed V

Trik el Koutoubia

Place de
Bâb Fteuh

Rue des
Banques

Rue el Moulay Ismail

**Place
Djamaâ
el-Fna**

Square de
Foucauld

Rue Riad Zitoun el Kedim

Avenue El Gadissia

Casino

Rue Haroun
ar Rachid

**Mosquée
Koutoubia**

Rue Bab Agnaou

Rue Moulay Ismail

Rue Riad Zitoun el Jedid

**Musée
Dar Si Saïd**

Bâb Aghmat

Avenue du Président Kennedy

Avenue El Gadissia

Avenue Houman el Fetouaki

Pl. Youssef
Ben Tachfine

Avenue Houmman el Ftouaki

**Palais
al-Bahia**

Rue Iman el Ghezali

Zaouiya de
Sidi Youssef
Ben Ali

Bâb
el Jédid

La Mamounia

Mausolée

Rue Ibn Rachid Avenue

Place des
Ferblantiers

MELLAH

**Jardin
Ménara**

Avenue de la Ménara

Bâb ech
Charia

Mosquée de
la Kasba

Bâb Berrima

Palais al-Badii

Sidi es
Souheyli

**Bâb
Agnaou**

**Tombeaux
Saâdiens**

Mosquée
Derb el Badi

Bâb er
Robb

**Mosquée
al-Mansour**

Palais Royal

Oliveraie

de Bab Jédid

Rue de la Kasba

Méchouar
extérieur

Rue de Bâb Ahmar

Bâb Ahmar

0   100 200 300 400 500 m

Méchouar
intérieur

Bâb Ksiba

**Jardin

Agdal**

Bâb Ighli

Rue de Bâb Ighli

Grand
Méchouar